The Blessings Book

Written by

Sarah Renee

Published by AuthorsUnite.com

Dedication

This book is dedicated to the people who have helped support me throughout my own spiritual healing journey. My family: Mom, Dad, and Lily. My best friend and my second family — Katie, Susan, Justin, Grant, Gracie, Finley, and Liberty. My Uncle Bob. My dear friend and photographer Kim Bajorek — who took the bio photo in the back of this book. My spiritual advisors and mentors — Catherine Yunt and Chris Marmes, God, the Universe, and my Spirit Team. All of my clients — I continue to learn so much from doing your readings and seeing your transformations. You inspire me daily and you helped inspire this book.

To everyone who has ever felt alone, weird, unworthy, and misunderstood. It can be hard walking this path, feeling everything in life so deeply. You are here to help wake up the world. I understand you. You were created perfectly just as you are and don't let anyone tell you differently. I appreciate your presence in the world and just know that when you tap into your inner connection, no amount of human disapproval can take away that Divine Love, the Universe's Approval. Remember that.

Contents

Foreword to The Blessings Book

At the end of August of 2015, I experienced the sudden, unexpected and agonizing loss of my father, Dr. Wayne Dyer. Everything in my life came to a halt as I grappled with how to carry on and pick up the pieces after my father, who was also my closest friend and employer, was gone in an instant. For those of you who do not know of him, he was a well-known author and speaker on all topics relating to spirituality and self-development, but for me, he was more than that. He was the voice of reason that I relied upon in all instances in my life. When I received the call that he had died unexpectedly in the middle of the night, I became acutely aware of a strong desire to reconnect with him now that he had transitioned to the world of spirit, and I immediately began talking to him in my mind and asking him to guide me, to somehow give me a sign, or a message that would assure that all of his life-teachings were right; meaning that the soul really does live on after it leaves the physical body it incarnated into during this lifetime. I began the process of meditation so that I could quiet my mind and allow his voice to come to me, and as I did that, the signs and messages from him began to come flooding in. One of the ways I was able

to reconnect with him, after he passed, was through gifted mediums or spiritual guides that randomly entered my life, seemingly at the exact moment I needed, and that is how I came to know Sarah Renee.

As I mentioned, my dad was a well-known individual in the world of spiritual teachings, so as one might expect, many individuals began reaching out to my family and me, offering "messages" from my dad. Truth be told however, most of these signs or messages did not resonate with me and I felt myself growing increasingly weary whenever someone indicated they could communicate with loved ones who had past and had a special message from my dad. That was not the case with Sarah Renee. From our first encounter, I sensed an authenticity, and her messages were specific and personal, so much so that I began to view her as one of only a handful of spiritual teachers or psychics or mediums if you will, that could really communicate with my father, and as time would prove, with other loved ones who passed as well.

When Sarah Renee began discussing her idea of writing The Blessings Book, I actually asked her if I could be so honored as to write the Foreword, something I had never actively sought out doing before, simply because I believed in her gifts so much that I wanted to help her get her work out there in any way that I could.

One of the things that I love about The Blessings Book, and Sarah Renee as an individual, is that she approaches the world of spiritual teachings from a completely judgement-

free mentality. As you will see as you begin to explore her book, Sarah Renee encourages each reader to adopt the practice of getting quiet, meditating, praying, or just quieting the mind not from a "one-size-fits-all" mentality that is so common amongst spiritual teachers, but instead, she teachers the reader to use the method or words or practice that is most comfortable for each individual, and emphasizes how important it is for the reader to do what is right for them. I love this approach as truth be told, each of us has our own journeys and our own beliefs, and instead of preaching that her way is the only way, or that you must follow her guidance exactly, she gently nudges each reader to follow the calling of their soul in order to connect with the spiritual world that is available to each of us at all times.

Throughout The Blessings Book, Sarah Renee offers practical and realistic ways that each of us can use to reconnect with our true purpose on this earth during this lifetime. Sarah Renee provides examples of her own mantras, prayers and practices that she uses, all while encouraging each of us to go within and find what works for us on a personal level as well. My favorite part of The Blessings Book are the examples that she provides of what it is she says or repeats in her own mind in order to call upon the angels and guides, or God, if that is what you prefer to call this mystical and omniscient force. As I read her words I am reminded of how important it is to be open to receiving guidance from the world beyond, I am reminded that all I have to do is ask, and then let go and receive.

What you are holding in your hands is a true gift offered to us, the reader, from a woman who has spent her life learning how to connect with the divine world of beyond. I am so excited for everyone who gets a copy of this book and I am thrilled for the adventure of personal growth and development that this book will gently nudge you on.

Serena Dyer

Introduction

This book is a creation of Spirit. It is a divine manuscript of prayers, rituals, mantras, meditations, and visualizations brought through from Spirit in order to help those reading these pages live a life feeling fully connected, supported, and in flow with their own divine essence. I have spent years working with people from all over the world, people of different faiths, backgrounds, languages, and circumstances. This book is inspired by them, as well as by the messages I have been honored to deliver. I have felt called to put together these powerful prayers and rituals in a way that anyone can relate to and use. You will notice throughout this book that I use the terms God, Spirit, Universe, Creator, Angels, and Guides all interchangeably. To me, they are all the same. I invite you to substitute the name which you refer to your Higher Power and any terms that feel most comfortable to you. I also use different words to seal in the prayers and mantras such as Amen, OM, And So It Is, and Thank you. Feel free to use whatever term best resonates for you. These prayers, rituals, and mantras have been channeled to compliment any religion or upbringing, and are designed to be used either word for word or modified to fit your unique beliefs. There are also several powerful

visualizations included. I tell my clients when practicing a visualization to follow that inner guidance if you see something different that suits you more. I believe it is more about establishing our own unique practices, beliefs, and connection rather than following a script written by someone else. The channeled messages in this book will help provide an introduction to your intuition, to your personal guidance system, and help your individual connection with God and Spirit unfold at a deeper level. The way Spirit gave me this information was divided into sections around calling in specific blessings into your life, hence the name, The Blessings Book. I believe that everyone has their own Spirit Team, a combination of loved ones in the afterlife, Guides, Angels, and Divine Beings. Calling on your Spirit Team for assistance on a daily basis will help guide your actions and words, while also setting up opportunities and circumstances that will help you live your best possible life. There is not a magic answer for making millions of dollars while sitting on your sofa watching TV, but I do believe that working with Spirit can make life not only easier, but more fulfilling, purposeful, and supportive. When we live from a place of knowing that we're on the right path, knowing that we're supported from something bigger than us, knowing that things are coming together, we experience this feeling of being in the flow. A feeling of momentum and trust. That is what this book is designed to help you achieve. I have also included chapters on healing because what Spirit shows me is that the more we hold onto residual trauma and

resentment, we become blocked like a clogged drain. By doing the healing work in this book, we can clear the blockage to make room for the blessings to enter. I hope this work adds as much goodness and happiness to your life as it has to mine and to my clients. Enjoy!

Chapter 1

Sacred Time and Space

You are a sacred being. It is vital to your existence to consciously create sacred time and a sacred space. You don't have to go crazy, even five minutes of sacred time per day can start to make a huge difference. By taking some time to clear your energy, be quiet, breathe, say some of the prayers or mantras in this book, you are giving yourself the time to connect with not only yourself but with your Higher Power. By taking even five minutes, you are declaring, "This is a priority for me and I am making the time." By getting quiet, you are training yourself to listen. The prayers and mantras in this book double in power when you say them. Take a few minutes to meditate on the thought that arises, or ask for guidance around that area. By saying a prayer and then taking some quiet time, you are creating space for an actual conversation with Spirit. You are taking the time to not only tell God, "This is what I want," but to listen to what God has to say to you. It also helps you start to learn what your body has to say to you, what your higher self has to say to you. By

spending a few minutes each day in this sacred space, it opens up another level of communication within yourself.

Another practice to produce profound results is setting up a sacred space, like an altar. I even set them up when I travel and am in hotel rooms. It doesn't have to be super fancy. If you set aside a small table or area and put out some symbols of God and the divine to you, maybe photos of your loved ones who are in Heaven, and something that feels like an offering, like flowers, or a pretty, decorated box, that's really all you need. Then you can use this space to put letters addressed to your Spirit Team, or things you need God to help take care of for you. It's a great place to put a vision board or vision journal, or symbols of what you want to call into your life. Make this space feel sacred and offer gratitude to your Spirit Team for blessing this space and all that you place in it. It's important to keep it clean and decluttered, and really take care of this space as you would any sacred ground. If you're working on yourself, maybe include a photo of yourself looking peaceful and happy or some quality you're wanting to possess and place it on your altar with your Team as a way of calling in those qualities. You can use a decorated box as a sort of "God Box." I first heard the term God Box at a twelve-step retreat, and I fell in love with the concept. You write down any situation that you've been obsessing over or worrying about or the names of any people you have a conflict with, and you place the paper inside the God Box, and let God sort it out. It helps a lot, and I found it to be extra powerful when I placed the God Box

on my altar. I keep a St. Michael statue, an image of Jesus, a Mother Mary statue, along with images of Mary Magdalene and the Goddess Brigid on my altar along with a photo of my Grandmother who passed when I was little, and my best friend who passed away several years ago. Any time I feel discouraged or alone, I sit in front of my altar and connect with them, then I'll write a letter and place it in the box. I am still amazed at how fast they can find solutions for things! You can also write down any of the following mantras or prayers that you want to continually work on, place it on your altar, and then spend some sacred time in front of it each day, repeating the prayer or mantra and connecting with Spirit. Creating a ritual around praying and meditating can help boost connection to your Higher Power and also ease your mind by giving you an "action step" to take each day. I invite you to try to bring this sacred energy into your life as much as you can, it may just help you remember your own sacredness and divinity.

In addition to prayers, mantras, and affirmations, I wanted to include crystals at the end of each chapter that can help support you. Crystals and stones have a unique energetic make up and frequency, and when you hold them during meditation, carry them in your pockets, or sleep with them under your pillow, they can help align your energy with the frequencies they naturally hold. When you go crystal shopping, I encourage you to be open to which types of crystals/stones you are naturally drawn to- usually you'll feel

called to pick up the one you need most- or you can purchase the ones suggested in these chapters.

♦ Crystals for Sacred Space or meditation: Amethyst, Selenite, Moonstone, Auralite, Lemurian Quartz

Chapter 2

Connecting With and Building Trust in Your Personal Spirit Team

I see a "team" of beings around every single person I meet whether I read them or not. We all have them watching over us. However, we also have free will. If we aren't giving our spirit team permission to intervene on behalf of our highest and best good, then they can try their best to protect us, but they can't fully force us to change our path. Have you ever had a bad gut feeling about something, only to push it aside because logically it seemed fine and then something went wrong or didn't work out? That's an example of free will and our logical mind overpowering our intuitive guidance from our Spirit team. It happens to all of us at some point or another. Occasionally, another person's free will can interject into our lives and cause harm or trauma, but consistently asking our Spirit Team for help and following their guidance can steer us out of harm's way the the majority, if not all, of the time. The following prayers, mantras, meditations, and visualizations are to help you

connect with your personal Spirit team, discover your personal signs, and ask them for help.

* Prayers, Affirmations, Mantras, and Visualizations *

God, please help me connect with You, my Guides, Angels, and loved ones more clearly. Please help me feel safe to receive the loving signs and messages that are around me. Please only allow forms of Spirit that are in your love and light to connect with me. Please help me be willing to allow their guidance into my heart. Thank you. Amen.

Spirit Team, I now give you permission to intervene on behalf of my highest and best good. Thank you. Amen. OM.

Universe, please give me a sign that you are supporting me, and if I'm on the wrong path, please give me a crystal clear sign to redirect me to a path that is in my highest and best good. I ask that you now show me the signs you use to tell me things clearly and repeatedly so that I may learn what to watch out for. I am paying attention. Thank you!

Angels, please help me feel you around me. Help me feel your light and your love. Help me feel you in a way that is undeniable, real and that will help me learn how to connect with you more often. Please help me to feel safe connecting with you, and keep me safe from any harsh energy. Thank you. Amen. OM.

God, Please show me Your will for me. Please guide me throughout my day so that my thoughts, words, and actions may align with your purpose for me. Send me the strength to fulfill my mission here. I now graciously accept the path You have cleared for me. I open to Your divine power now. I remember that I have Your essence within me at all times. May I live each day aligned with Thy Will Be Done. May You guide me in all that I do. Thank you. Amen. OM.

I am now being divinely guided in all of my decisions. I trust that God, the Universe, and Spirit are watching over me. I am safe.

I know that I was created on purpose. I am here for a reason and the Universe is guiding me in fulfilling my Soul's highest purpose here. I now trust my inner guidance system.

I listen to my intuition and know that I am being taken care of.

I now have the courage to follow my inner voice.

I am now in tune with my Spirit Team. I hear them, feel them, and receive their messages with love, ease, and confidence.

Visualizations

Imagine a bubble of white, gold, green, blue, or pink light around you. Whichever color calls to you the most. Now imagine this bubble getting bigger and bigger. See Angels and divine beings around you,

sending healing, divine light into this bubble, filling you and your energy field up with their essence. Feel the safety, calmness, and trust of being in this light. You can keep this bubble of light around you all day and all night. It will help keep you clear and centered.

◆ Crystals for connecting with Spirit: Amethyst, Lemurian Quartz, Moldavite, Celestite

Chapter 3

Safety, Security, and Well-Being

The Ego can create a lot of fear, and we can also pick up on global fear that may be holding us back from living a happy life. It is our Universal right to have safety, security, and well-being in our lives. By allowing your Spirit Team to help you with these basic needs, you can not only experience peace on a daily basis, but you will start to feel the abundance and support of the divine flowing through you and the fear and anxiety will fade away. The following are prayers, mantras, and visualizations to help with fear, anxiety, housing situations, and finances.

✱ Prayers, Affirmations, Mantras, and Visualizations ✱

My Creator, I call on You now to protect me from all harm. Please remove all abuse, negative energy, daggers, black magic, and/or any toxic energy sent my way, please send it into the light for transmutation. Please help repair and rebuild my energy field where any damage has been done. I give you permission to cut all toxic cords that have been draining me. Please intervene on behalf of my well being. Please keep me safe. Thank you. I love you. Amen. OM.

God, Angels, and Guides, I open my arms to you and allow myself to receive your blessings. I am ready for all the good you have in store for me. I can feel your abundance raining down on me now. I accept it gratefully into my heart, my bank account, and my life. Thank you for teaching me how to receive gracefully. I promise to continue to do good and to pay it forward with all of the blessings you bestow upon me. I will gladly serve as a vessel of prosperity, overflowing and radiate abundance for everyone around me. Thank you! I love you! Amen. And so it is.

God, Please cleanse me of all fear, worry, obsession, and anxiety. I ask that You now fill me with your healing light and Grace. That You now remind me of my own God/Goddess essence. Please align my entire being with peace, clarity, and faith now. Help me center and ground into Your love for me. Thank you. Amen.

Angels, please take away any and all fear, anxiety, and doubt and send it into the light to be healed and transmuted. Please replace those thoughts with healing, peace, trust, and clarity. Thank you. Amen.

Spirit Team, I ask you to please show me the underlying cause of my fear and anxiety. Is there something I need to be aware of? Please show me the best action to take right now in order to heal and feel safe. Help me move forward peacefully. Thank you!

God, I ask that you bring Your divine peace and harmony into this situation. Please help everyone involved come together and find a solution for the highest and best good. Thank you!

Universe, I now call upon peace and healing. I ask that my mind, heart, and body be filled with peace and that I now am centered in my natural, grounded energy. Thank you!

God and Angels, please clear me of all external energy and return it to its sender with love and compassion. Thank you!

God, Please help me feel safe, supported, and cared for. Please help guide me to a living environment that is in my highest and best good. Please allow me to live somewhere that is happy, healthy, and fully aligned for me. A place where I can be in the flow of all good things. I surrender my living situation to You and I will follow the signs You leave for me to get there. Thank You for always taking care of me. I know You've got this handled. Amen.

Angels, Please fill my home with love, peace, serenity, abundance, and health. Feel free to add some joy and extra blessings on top of that! I give you permission to clear away all negative energy that no longer serves me. I now see my home radiating your divine light. Thank you!!!

Archangel Michael, please keep my home, my family, and me safe. Please shield us from any harsh energy. Please clear away all toxic or harmful energies and replace them with your divine light, power, and love. Please place Angel Guards at all doors and windows to allow only love and goodwill in. Thank you! I love you! Amen.

Angels, please help me keep me safe and help me feel your protection around me now! Thank you!

I am fully taken care of at all times.

The Universe is providing for me.

I am wealthy, healthy, and happy!

I am being guided to the perfect living situation for me. God's got it, I can let go.

It's all working out in my highest and best good.

I am safe.

Visualizations

Imagine inhaling in white light, from the Divine realms, through the crown of your head, pause in your

heart. Exhale that light down, out of your feet into the earth. Inhale that light up from the earth, pause in your heart. Exhale up to the divine realms. Continue this breathing and visualizing this light clearing you of all fear, negativity, toxic energy, and healing your entire body and energy field as it moves through you. You can practice expanding the light out of you, even directing it out of your hands to fill up your entire home. You can also visualize the light coming from an Angel, Jesus, or other divine figure standing behind you with their hands either on your shoulder blades or the top of your head. This can help you feel safe, and will also clear your energy.

If you are wanting to call in a new living arrangement, this next visualization is extra powerful! Close your eyes and see yourself in your new home. What does it feel like? What does it look like? What sounds do you hear? What do you smell? What colors are the walls? How is it designed? Where is it? Walk through your home, imagine running your hands along the furniture or countertops, imagine looking out the windows at the view. See what your life is like there. Be there, in that space. Make it as real as possible. Practice this daily to help align you with the energy of your new home.

Money Visualization:

This is great to do when you're laying in bed in the morning and evening. Imagine money raining down on you. Imagine little Angels, Fairies, and/or your

loved ones from the other side bringing you cash, placing it underneath your pillow, in your pockets, in your wallets or purse. Imagine them stuffing it under your mattress. Don't think about where it's coming from, just focus on them delivering it to you and letting yourself fully receive it. Then affirm to yourself, money is coming to me and flowing through me now. Money is everywhere and comes to me in multiple ways. I am making more and more money every single day.

♦ Crystals for Safety and Security: Citrine, Selenite, Garnet, Ruby, and Jasper

Chapter 4

Self Love, Acceptance, and Forgiveness

What holds a lot of people back from receiving blessings in life is a deep sense of unworthiness. Feeling unworthy can also cause health issues, relationship issues, depression, and a feeling of disconnection. Your Spirit Team wants you to know that you are worthy of divine care and love. You were sent here to be alive right now for a reason. You are on purpose. You belong. And you were created perfectly with all that you need to succeed.

✳ Prayers, Affirmations, Mantras, and Visualizations ✳

God, please help release me from the bondage of self-hate, sabotage, shame, and blame. Please clear me of all negative belief systems and self-abuse that I have running on autopilot. Please replace my negative thought patterns with loving guidance from You. Please help me see myself the way that You see me. Thank you. Amen. Angels, please clear me from all old behaviors, patterns, addictions, and negative choices that have been holding me back. Help me release all self-defeat, and program me for success, love, healing, and positive life choices now. Help me show up as my best self. Thank you! Amen.

God, please clear all old verbal and emotional abuse from my mind. Please stop those voices from running my life and remind me of what's true. Replace those voices with the voice of You, my loved ones on the other side, and my Spirit Team. Help me hear loving and supportive messages. Thank you!

Universe, please re-align my energy with love, worthiness, and success. Restructure my path from lack and unworthiness, to a life better than I could ever even imagine. Thank you!

Angels, please help show me loving and accepting relationships with everyone I come into contact with. Help me feel the unconditional love and support You have for me. Show me how to care for myself in a gentle, loving way. Show me I am worthy of receiving good experiences and care in my life. Thank you! Amen.

God, help me laugh more! Please take this heaviness from my heart and fill me with joy, bliss, and laughter. Remind me of my inner lightness. Thank you!

God, help me see my divinity. Show me my sacredness, restore my magic. Let me see myself as holy. Let me see myself as an expression of Your essence. Help me see my true self. Amen. OM.

I am worthy.

I deserve to be happy now.

The past is done, and I now release it with love. I know I did my best, and I release myself from the prison of shame. I love myself. I now claim the life I know I deserve.

I release all self-pity and stand in my own love, courage, and worthiness.

I am a sacred, holy being of light. And So It Is.

Dear Self, I forgive you for those mistakes you made before. I know now that you were doing the best that you knew how to do. I am so sorry that I spent so long beating you up for it, but I promise that as of now, I will no longer talk to you with hate or anger. I love you so much. You deserve to live a long, happy life, and I can now help you get there. We are being taken care of now, and being shown the way. We're safe. It's okay to put down all of that stuff that happened in the past. You learned the lessons, there's no need to carry it forward. It's okay now. You are worthy of healing.

Visualizations

Close your eyes and imagine yourself at whatever age you were when you started to feel unworthy. Get a clear picture of that version of yourself in your head. Look at the circumstances you were dealing with. Start to see that part of yourself with compassion and empathy. See that you were doing the best you could. Imagine reaching out, taking your hand, and telling yourself, "It's okay, I can take care of you now. You did your best, and I know that. There is no need to feel ashamed. I love you." Pull them into you and imagine them merging with who you are now. You can also ask what that part of you needs that maybe they missed out on, and try to spend some time doing activities that nurture them. For example, if it's a child self, maybe spend time coloring or playing outdoors. As you integrate and care for those parts of you, the shame

will disappear. You are the one who decides you're worthy, and the key to believing you are worthy is showing yourself you are worthy. Another powerful exercise is to write yourself a letter and Makepeace with yourself over whatever happened in the past. Forgive that part of you, have compassion for them, validate them, and give them permission to come to be with you in your life now and stop holding onto the things holding you back. Set them free. Close your eyes and start to visualize your ideal self. This may come across to you as your higher self or future self, as long as it feels true for you, that's what's important. See yourself showing up in this visualization as the best version of you. As you embodying your full potential. How does that part of you feel? What are you doing? Where are you? How are you dressed? Follow this part of you around a little bit. Notice how your relationships are, how you carry yourself, what you're doing for work or hobbies, how you take care of yourself, what fun you're having, where you live, what you drive, etc. Notice as many details about yourself as possible. Now, imagine walking up to this version of you, as the you that you are today. Give this part of you a big hug, congratulating them on how far they've come and how amazing they are, and then imagine both versions of you merging together, and bringing that ideal self into your present self. When you open your eyes, write down as much as you can

remember about that part of yourself. And set an intention to express that part of you a little more every day. Maybe you start doing some of the activities from your visualization, or begin to dress and behave as your visualized self. Then take simple steps to make positive changes in your life. This will help you show up as your best self every single day, and eventually, it will become your new normal!

◆ Crystals for Self-love, forgiveness, and acceptance: Rose Quartz, Green Calcite, Green Flourite, Rhodonite

Chapter 5

Healing from Trauma

When I do readings or healing sessions with people, I see trauma stored in their physical and energetic body. I will see it in different forms, sometimes it looks like black dirt or thick dust, sometimes it's a thick, tar-like rope or cord, and other times it looks like a large mass of a tar type substance. It's usually very sticky, thick, and dark. The dirt or dust is usually when most of the trauma has been cleared, but there are still remnants of that energy. I also sometimes see the energy from the person or situation that inflicted the trauma still lingering within my client, or a cord still attaching them. It's important to heal trauma and PTSD on all levels, mental, emotional, physical, and energetically. What also happens with trauma, is some of our energy gets taken by the person or situation that caused the original trauma. I see this as a ball of light, usually representing the power of the person traumatized, that has been removed from them and is being held at either a location or within the perpetrator. This causes a lot of people to feel fragmented, or like a part of them is forever missing, which is why it's so important to reclaim

that energy. I will include two visualizations in this chapter, one for clearing their energy, and one for reclaiming your energy. I recommend practicing both. Also, something I've found to be extremely powerful is taking these prayers and writing them as letters to God and Spirit, and then expanding and telling them exactly what you need help releasing and asking for that healing and peace.

* Prayers, Affirmations, Mantras, and Visualizations *

God, please help me recover from this situation. I call upon You to clear me from this dark, negative energy. I ask You to take this pain, violence, anger, and hurt, and transmute it into something good. If anyone can do so, I know You can. Please guide me in transforming this experience of being victimized into something healing and empowering. Show me how to use this experience for Good and please keep me safe. Thank you!

Angels, please clear me of any belief systems around identifying this traumatic experience as who I am. Help me remember who I truly am, and clear out that fear-based energy. Please send all lingering energy from this event into the light to be cleared and transmuted. Please send any energy absorbed from others associated with this trauma back to them, please cut all toxic cords formed during this event, and restore me to my highest and best self. I give You permission to take the heaviness of this event off my shoulders and send it into the light. I am willing to be set free from this and fulfill my highest purpose here. Thank you! Amen. OM.

Dear Self, it was not your fault. You did the best that you could do in that situation. It is time to let go of the self-blame. It is over, and you are free. I love you. Let me take care of you. Let God take care of us. And so it is.

I now release any and all thought patterns associated with, "I have to be on guard, it could happen again, I deserved it, I will never be safe," and any other thoughts or belief systems around this trauma that come to mind. I command that these thought patterns be replaced with, "I am safe, I deserve safety, security, and happiness. I am still sacred and holy. I love myself, I am loved by God, my Angels, and the Universe. I am free to start over, I am powerful. I command that I am now healed within and without. Amen. OM." And so it is.

I now give myself full permission to release all flashbacks, replays, and cycles of fear associated with this trauma. I trust that I learned all I needed to from this experience and by releasing these reminders I know I will not release the ultimate lessons. This experience does NOT define me. I am safe now.

I deserve to heal.

It is safe for me to be happy again.

It is safe for me to trust myself.

I am whole.

I am STILL a sacred being of light.

I am strong. I am brave. I am courageous.

I am me. I am not defined by this, but rather I am defined by how I show up in my life every day. I am defined by who I choose to be, not by what another person forced upon me. I have the power to release their projections and reclaim my own identity. I am free.

Visualization for Clearing Trauma:

Ask that you be surrounded in white light and that this healing is in your highest and best good. Imagine lying down on a healing bed. There are Angels all around you. Call upon any Angels or divine figures that you work with regularly. Now, see these Angels and Guides sending you swirls of healing light. The light is filled with light golds, white, pink, blues, greens, all nurturing colors. This light swirls around your feet, and winds up and around your body, creating a cocoon of healing. As it swirls up and around you, the Angels send the healing light through the crown of your head, into your body. Imagine it gathering up any dark energy associated with trauma, moving it into a sphere of energy near your low belly. The light moves through your entire body, sweeping this energy from every cell, every corner, gathering up every ounce of trauma. When this energy is completely gathered, the Angels place their hands over your belly and they pull this dark mass of energy out of you, sending it into the light to be fully cleared and transmuted. They immediately send healing light into your body to repair anywhere that was holding this darkness. The Angels cut any cords connected to the location of the trauma,

and to any other people involved. They gather up any energy lingering from those people or locations and send that energy back to where it came from. They fill you up with healing, loving light, replenishing every cell of your body, filling up your energy field, and shielding you from any further traumatic situations. They secure you in this light so that the healing may continue even after this visualization. Give a thank you to your Angels, Guides, and to yourself for receiving this healing and practicing this visualization.

Visualization for Reclaiming Your Energy:

Imagine you're standing in a comfortable room, surrounded by your Angels, Guides, and loved ones. Feel the light, the warmth, and the unconditional love in that room. Feel yourself fully protected, fully safe. Now, look in front of you and see a big wall of glass. The glass is very strong, nothing can get through it. Your Angels assure you that you are safe as you walk towards the glass. Now you see any person, people, or places that have caused you harm, or that have contributed to trauma on the other side of this glass. They aren't able to reach through the glass or even speak through the glass. They are not able to get to you. Your Angels assure you that you are in control here. As you look at them through the glass, you see a little ball of light in them, a ball of your energy that they took during the traumatic incident. Your Angels show you that it is time to take that energy back. They help you reach through the glass, and as you hold your palm up, light reflects out of it like a magnet and your energy

and power that was being held in the person or location comes straight back to you, you hold it in your hand, and bring it back through the glass. Your Angels hold their hands over yours, sending healing into that energy, restoring it to be fully aligned with you, and then you re-install it back to yourself through the crown of your head, your heart, or your lower belly. As you breathe, you fully integrate that energy and power back within yourself, and you see your Angels carry those people off into the light, out of your energy field. You know it is done. Now, you are whole again.

♦ Crystals for healing from trauma: Rhodonite, green calcite, orange calcite, kunzite, kyanite, lepidolite

Chapter 6

Passion, Creativity, Sexuality

I see a lot of clients who feel like they're simply going through the motions. Their life isn't terrible, but they've lost that sense of passion, curiosity, and their aliveness. They experience a block in their creativity, and many feel disconnected from their sexual essence or are feeling unfulfilled in their intimate relationships. The good news is, Spirit can help here, too! It's amazing how many people forget or don't feel like these areas are important enough to pray for help in, but they are! Spirit says the more you are living your life passionately and engaged, the more impact you have on people around you. The more you are raising the collective vibration, the happier you start to become, the happier everyone else starts to become, then you all start inspiring others to connect with their passions, and so on. For you to live in joy, bliss, to be passionate, to be able to express yourself creatively, to be turned on and feel a sense of desire within yourself and your relationships. It is

absolutely important, and most of all, it's part of why you came here! You came here to enjoy life, to enjoy helping others, to enjoy expressing your divine nature through a physical body.

* Prayers, Affirmations, Mantras, and Visualizations *

God, please fill me with a sense of passion again. Remind me what it feels like to feel enthusiastic and fully alive! Please restore the passion in my relationships, and help connect me with like-minded people. I am ready to enjoy life again! Thank you! Amen.

Angels, please help free my creative energy. Let it flow through me now, unrestricted, unedited, wild and free as it was meant to. Help me create with an open mind, spirit, and soul. Help me create from my heart. Thank you!

Angels and Guides, please guide me in ways to express myself creatively. Help me find activities that will boost my own creativity and help me release my emotions. Give me the courage to express myself freely and openly. Thank you!

Angels, please help me to heal my sexuality. Help me to see my sexual nature as a gift, and as a divine part of me. Please clear me of any negativity associated with sexuality, intimacy, or passion. Please clear me of any shame around my sexuality or past sexual encounters. Please guide me in creating a healthy, passionate, sacred, safe sexual intimacy with my partner, and/or within myself. Thank you. Amen.

Goddess Pele, Goddess of Passion, please awaken my inner passion. Please direct me towards experiences, people, or things that will spark my inner passion and desire. Remind me what my Soul truly craves. Help me to experience pleasure in all areas of my life. Thank you! Amen. And so it is.

God, please help me feel my emotions fully, in a way that is safe and not too overwhelming. Please help me feel and process these emotions in a healthy way. Guide me to creative outlets that will help validate and clear me of any emotions that I've kept repressed or buried. Teach me to handle my emotions with ease and grace rather than escapism. Thank you! Amen.

It is safe for me to be desirable.

It is safe for me to experience pleasure, bliss, and ecstasy. God created me to experience pleasure. It is my divine right to feel passion, desire, craving, and bliss.

I now release any and all vows of celibacy from any past lives. I release all shame associated with my sexuality or with sexual pleasure.

I now decide to reignite my passion and take life as my lover.

I give myself permission to create freely.

I now let my creative energy flow through me, in any way it wants to be expressed. I give myself permission to feel my emotions fully, to express them, and to be fully seen and heard.

Visualization:

Music is actually a great tool for your creativity, emotions, and sexuality. Listening to music and dancing around your house, specifically moving your hips, will loosen up any blocked creative energy, passion, or sexual tension.

Visualize yourself in a safe space. Maybe you're on an island somewhere, and only you control who is allowed there. Imagine bringing in whoever you choose to. Imagine all of your senses taking in pleasure. Smelling fragrant flowers or the ocean, or maybe the mountain air, or delicious food cooking. Feeling soft fabric on your skin, or a cool or warm breeze on your skin. See beautiful scenery all around and the people that you love. Imagine you've just succeeded at helping out a cause that you're super passionate about, and this is your celebration. Taste food or drinks that you can savor and enjoy. Imagine the sounds you enjoy in the Background such as music, nature, people, etc. The main focus in this visualization is to stimulate all of your senses and allow yourself to fully enjoy and partake in that

pleasure and celebration. Come back to your present reality and set the intention to bring this passion into your current life, then look for ways you can bring those experiences to life each day. If we all did one thing daily that were passionate about, people would be a lot happier!

♦ Crystals for Passion, Creativity, and Sexuality: orange carnelian, orange calcite, blue calcite, citrine

Chapter 7

Personal Power, Divine Power, Action

Power is actually quite a complex topic. I have worked with many people who are afraid to step into their power, afraid of how others will view them, afraid of abusing their power, afraid it will be taken away once they claim it. I've worked with those who feel completely powerless. I've worked with people who were so focused on being in a place of power it actually sabotaged their life. In my personal life, I spent years fluctuating between a place of feeling so powerful I thought I was invincible, to total powerlessness and victimhood. I finally landed in the magic zone that I refer to as Divine Power, and that is where I focus on helping my clients and students get to. Divine Power is when we actually link up our personal power, and our personal will, with our Creator's will for us, and with the power of God/Spirit/Universe, which is so much bigger than any human power. When you are living in a place of Divine Power, you will feel protected, inspired, motivated,

supported, and like you're being taken care of. It's an interesting dichotomy of feeling in charge, but not in control. It's like you know you're not in control, and in that surrender, you access this power that is greater than anything you've ever experienced. When we stop spending our energy on trying to control everything, we have infinite energy to invest in the things that actually matter like taking actions toward our life purpose, loving each other, spreading kindness, etc. The example that Spirit shows me is near the core of our body: our stomach and mid-back area where we can actually receive a cord of energy from our Angels, our Spirit Teams, God, etc. They send in their willpower, their strength, their power, to merge and integrate with our own willpower and strength, and when these two sources of power are combined, we can do anything! The following prayers, mantras, and visualization are to help with accessing that Divine Power, taking divinely guided action, and to know what God's will for you is.

* Prayers, Affirmations, Mantras, and Visualizations *

God, please grant me the strength to show up in this situation in away that is empowering for myself and others. I am afraid I cannot make it on my own, so I pray that You fill me with Your power, love, and care now. Please guide my actions and help me make the best choices towards the best possible solution. Thank you! Amen.

Angels, I call on you now and ask that you fill me with courage, inspiration, and motivation to take the necessary steps to move forward. Please show me what I need to see and help guide me on this path. I give you permission to intervene in my daily actions and conversations in order to align them with my highest and best good. Please let your divine power flow through me now and move me in the direction I am meant to go in. Thank you!

God, please reveal to me YOUR WILL for me. Please show me what You will have me do here, who You will have me be. Please fill me with the power I need to accomplish your mission for me here. I give You permission to work your miracles and magic in my life. Thank you!

God, please work through me. Thank you! Spirit Team, please clear me of all energy and behaviors related to sabotage, failure, self-doubt, and weakness. I am ready to be who I truly am. Please restore my Divine Power, link my will to God's Will, and grant me the inner strength to succeed. I am ready. I am willing. I can do this. Thank you!

I now surrender my life to God's Will for me. I hand over every situation, relationship, and circumstance that I have gotten myself into so that God, my Angels, and Spirit can bring Divine Powerband Will in. I ask that Divine Will be done here. I am willing to give up control and take the actions needed. Guide me. Thank you!

I am a powerful being of light.

I have God's infinite power flowing through me.

I have Angels carrying me through this experience with grace and ease.

I am now restored to my ultimate Divine Power and am carrying out God's Will for me.

I am living my life purposefully. I am taking action, I am making a difference. I am showing up fully, every single day.

I now call back all power that I have given away to people or circumstance. I call back any and all power that has been taken from me. I call in the Power of the Universe. I step fully into this power, knowing that I am to use it for only good things. It is safe for me to be powerful now.

Visualization:

Visualize a cord, like an umbilical cord almost, attaching from the core of your physical body up to the Divine, to God, the Angels, the Universe, whatever your Higher Power is, and imagine this golden light flowing into you from the Divine, filling you with true power, with your ultimate purpose here, with God's Will for you. Imagine that same light merging with every cell of your body, giving youth strength, stamina, and confidence to take the actions needed. Imagine it filling up your energy field around your body, giving you warrior-like energy, protecting you,

and also emanating power, courage, and light. Feel this power leading you down your path, guiding all of your actions so that you may act in a way that is in your highest and best good. Feel this power carrying you through any type of conflict, so that you may handle whatever comes your way from a divine and powerful perspective. Feel this power as nurturing, unwavering, stable strength. There is no fear here, no need to intimidate or control. This power is trusting, kind, and comes from love. You can "plug into" this divine power source anytime you need an extra boost!

♦ Crystals for Will Power, Divine Power, and Action: carnelian, citrine, bloodstone, red jasper

Chapter 8

Self Expression and Speaking Your Truth

How often do you speak from your heart? How often do you speak from your Soul Self? I see so many cases of miscommunication coming from words said from a place of fear, anger, people-pleasing, or even just such an overly edited part of people's minds that they aren't able to get across what they really are feeling. Not being able to express yourself fully can lead to health issues around your throat, thyroid issues, and stiff muscles. It could also cause a general feeling of being stifled all the time, and deep-seated resentment from feeling unheard. Yes, sharing from your heart and soul can be terrifying at first, but Spirit can help us get through that fear and reach a place where that's how we speak all of the time. Now, this doesn't mean being so unedited that you speak in a way that is rude or hurtful. That is certainly not coming from your heart and soul, even if you are angry. Take the time to consciously choose your words, or ask God or your higher self to speak through you so that

every conversation is in everyone's highest and best good, even difficult and triggering ones. I find some of these prayers the most useful to say before a difficult conversation actually. Spirit has helped me express my feelings in ways that lead to solutions I could never have imagined on my own. I invite you to start this process simply by becoming aware of where you are talking from when you're speaking with people then ask yourself where you're listening from when you're hearing people. Are you in your Ego? That place of fear, judgment, control, attachment? Or, are you in your heart and soul, a place of genuine care and compassion, inner truth, kindness, and assertiveness? Just bringing that awareness into your conversations will have a huge impact!

✳ Prayers, Affirmations, Mantras, and Visualizations ✳

God, Angels, Guides, Spirit Team, I ask that You speak through me. Help direct my words so that I may be of maximum use at this moment. Grant me the courage to share openly. Thank you! Amen.

Angels, please guide my words and help me speak in a way that is in the highest and best good of everyone involved. Thank you! God, help me express my boundaries in a healthy way. God, help me hear this person's deepest truth. Help me see their perspective and guide me in showing them that they are heard.

Spirit Team, help me speak my truth and be heard at this moment. Guide my words in a way that allows me to ask clearly for what I need, in a way that is receptive to those I am speaking with. Help others hear my truth. Thank you. Amen.

God, please flow through me and guide me in speaking miracles into reality. And so it is. Universe, please open me up and allow me to express myself fully, clearly, and authentically. Thank you!

I feel the wisdom of a thousand wise ancestors flowing through me as I speak. May my words carry healing, depth, and comfort.

I feel Spirit guiding my words and I trust that everything I say is being divinely guided at this moment.

My words are magic.

I now give myself permission to fully express myself and be heard. My voice has the power to heal.

My voice has power.

I now choose to consciously release any and all stories, fears, or patterns that have been holding me back from speaking my truth. I give myself permission to fully express my truth. I now choose to honor my sacred voice -- my voice that speaks from the depths of my soul. My voice that expresses the truth running through my veins. My voice that tells no

lies. I honor my voice that creates my reality and embraces the infinite power of my words.

♦ Powerful crystals for speaking your truth: Lapis Lazuli, Azurite, and Aquamarine.

Chapter 9

Love and Relationships

Probably one of the most common reasons people come to me is requesting help either finding love or with a current relationship. I'm sure Spirit could send through an entire book on this area, but we'll try to squeeze it into one chapter. In relationships, Spirit says it's important to really see people as they are showing up, not as who you want them to be. Address things from that perspective. Also, good communication is vital. One of the most important factors in either calling in a new partner, or taking your current relationship to another level, is getting really clear on what it is that you actually want and desire, and coming into alignment with that. The visualization at the end of this chapter will be focused around that, and I invite you to write down your visualization after you go through it so you can reflect. Spirit says our relationships really reflect what's going on within us. So look at triggers and patterns as opportunities to address and heal that within yourself. I am

also going to include some prayers for healing after an abusive relationship and cutting cords. If you have been in an abusive situation, please get support for yourself and also refer back to the chapter on trauma. All abuse takes a toll and requires healing before you can get into a healthy relationship.

Prayers, Affirmations, Mantras, and Visualizations

God, help me see the wound being triggered by this situation, and guide me in how to best heal it. Thank you! Amen.

Spirit, help me see my part in this situation. How have my actions contributed, and how can I be a part of a solution?

God, show me the truth about this person and this relationship. I am willing to see the truth and follow Your guidance on what to do next. Thank you. Amen. Angels, please fill me up with your loving, pink light. Let this light flow through me, into the heart of my lover, and back through you. Let us be connected by divine love. Guide us in creating a deeper connection with one another on all levels. Thank you!

God, I now completely surrender my love life to You. I trust that You know what's best for me. Please guide me in moving forward, and show me a clear sign when someone is meant to be in my life. Thank you!

Spirit Team, please show me if this person is meant to be in my life or not. I give you permission to remove them if they no longer serve my highest good, or bring us closer together if that is what is meant to be. Thank you for taking care of me!

Spirit, please bring me into alignment with the relationship I desire. Help guide me in any adjustments that I need to make and help bring my person into my life. Thank you!

Universe, please show me what healthy, supportive, equal relationships look like. Thank you!

Archangel Michael, please cut any and all toxic cords between myself and _____. Please send all of their energy back to them, and return any energy of mine back to me, fully restored and repaired. Please send each of us love and compassion and allow us to part peacefully. Thank you!

Angels, please help me set healthy boundaries in this relationship. Guide me in speaking up, asking for what I need, and being the healthiest partner I can be. Thank you! Amen. God, help me be willing to open and experience equal, unconditional, romantic love.

God, help me to release all past relationships and stop me from projecting any past fears or experiences into this new relationship. Help me to be in a relationship as the person you meant for me to be. Thank you. Amen.

Angels, help me to feel safe enough to love again. I give you permission to bring into my life a person who will love me equally, who is emotionally available, attractive, stable, safe, in integrity, passionate, spiritually aligned with me, prosperous, consistent, patient, loyal, and healthy. (Feel free to adjust to fit your list of ideal qualities.) This or someone even better suited for me. I release it to you. Thank you! Amen.

I am a vessel of love and passion. I now let my heart shine out, creating a beam of light that filters in and attracts loving experiences.

I am love.

I sprinkle love everywhere I go.

My partner and I are now fully aligned and on the same page. Our hearts create magic in all of our endeavors together. We are supported by Spirit in creating a happy, passionate, successful, loving relationship with one another.

I now allow myself to be loved and adored fully, just as I am.

I am being guided to those who are safe to love.

I release all shame from past relationships or from loving too much. I know there is no such thing as too much love and I now call in a partner who matches my love equally.

I command that as of now I will no longer be desecrated, I shall be worshipped.

My lover and I are holy beings and every intimate moment is a sacred time where our Souls touch and we worship the God essence in one another. Our lovemaking is our prayer to the Holy Spirit that united us.

Visualization:

You can do this if you're single wanting to call in a relationship, or if you're coupled to see what you may be longing to create in your current relationship. Imagine your ideal day with your partner. Start from waking up and then go from there. What do you do? Where are you? How do you feel with this person? What's your life like? Let yourself go into full daydream mode, and then try to write as many details down as possible when you're done. Then take some time and ask yourself if you're living that lifestyle now, or if you're aligned with that lifestyle. What are some things you can start doing now, whether single or partnered? How can you bring those feelings into your life or current relationship? This second one is great for those in a relationship, especially if there have been arguments or if they aren't doing something you need. Visualize your current partner. See a clear image of them in your mind's eye. Imagine sending them love, giving them a hug. Tell them 'thank you' for all the things you love about them. Bring into your awareness all the reasons you're grateful for them. Everything that they do for you. Let yourself be in this

space of full appreciation and devotion to them as your lover. Send gratitude to them for being such an extraordinary partner. Imagine sending loving light into their heart. If you want to create more intimacy, imagine sending loving light into their second chakra region -- right around the hips and sexual organs then up to their heart and back through you, creating a loop of light connecting you both. After you're done, chances are the energy between you two will feel lighter and more loving. This can actually help them be willing to compromise or participate in a conversation from a calmer place, even though you didn't necessarily say it out loud. For couples really wanting to get on the same page again, a great practice that has worked well for couples who come to me is to combine this with actually sharing with your partner three things you appreciate the most about them every single day and have them do the same thing with you. It helps both people feel special, validated, and needed.

♦ Crystals for love and relationships are: Rose Quartz, Malachite, Opal, and Ruby.

Chapter 10

Health and Physical Healing

You've most likely heard the expression, "Your body is a temple", but how often do you truly live from that belief? Do you consistently treat your body like a temple, or do you beat it up from time to time? Do you praise and adorn your body, or do you ridicule it? Do you spend time clearing it out, or do you hold onto everything? Most disease originates as blocked energy according to the Guides. This is not to say there aren't physical elements, I am not a medical doctor, but I see the sickness in the body as something that begins as trapped or blocked energy, that then becomes disease or illness. A lot of times this energy that gets trapped are old wounds, traumas, resentments, or negative emotions that get repressed into the body. Combine that with chemicals and toxins absorbed through processed food or food that isn't organic, and you've got a perfect combination for illness. I am a big believer in combining Eastern and Western medicine, along with energetic healing to really work on

healing the body from all aspects. While these visualizations and meditations are not a substitute for medical care, I do recommend using them in addition to treatment and as prevention. When we are constantly clearing our bodies, bringing in healing, bringing our body into balance (processing and releasing old emotions) our body will be able to function at its best. Combine this work with a healthy diet of fresh, natural, organic foods, and you have a great combination for health and vitality!

* Prayers, Affirmations, Mantras, and Visualizations *

God, please fill my body with Your healing light and divinity. Please upgrade every cell to total health, vitality, and radiance. I now see myself as Your perfect, holy creation. I now fully integrate my sacredness and full physical potential. Thank you! Amen.

God, please remove any old, stagnant energy from my body and energy field. I give You permission to bring me into balance and raise my entire frequency. Please restore me to my ultimate healthy state. Thank you!

Angels, please cleanse me of all toxicity, negativity, and trauma. Please reset my entire being to harmony, safety, and peace. Thank you, Angels! And so it is.

Universe, please align me with perfect health, wholeness, and lightness. Bring my body into complete balance now. Help me function at my best. Thank you!

Angels, please fill me with your light and joy. I ask that you now restore my happiness. Fill my life with laughter, love, and purity. Remind me not to take things so seriously. Help me to lighten up! Thank you! Amen. OM.

I now give myself permission to restore to total and complete health. It is safe for me to be happy, healthy, and free. I fill my body with love and light, and I give thanks for this physical manifestation I chose this lifetime.

I now step into my full potential- physically, mentally, emotionally, and spiritually. I now embrace all aspects of myself. I now honor myself as the holy, divine being that I am. I now honor and recognize my inner light. I am ready to fulfill my divine mission.

I bring my body into balance with love and appreciation.

Dear Body, I am sorry for judging you so harshly. I apologize for the stress I have put you through, for the unhealthy toxins I have made you process, for not honoring you. I love you- exactly as you are. I thank you for being my vessel for this lifetime. I will take care of you now.

Visualizations:

Visualize inhaling a white and gold healing light from the Divine realms into the crown of your head and exhale it out of your feet and into the earth. Imagine this light pushing out any toxins, old energy, traumas, wounds, anything that no longer serves you- out

through your feet and into the earth for it to heal and transmute. Imagine this light healing every cell of your body, balancing you, clearing out any aches or pains, bringing your spine into total alignment, soothing your organs, clearing out any heaviness. When you feel complete, bring your awareness to your feet on the ground. Feel the support of the earth. Feel yourself being fully connected and grounded. Feel yourself aligning and coming into balance with the earth and with nature. This next visualization is for any discomfort, pain, illness, or if you've had physical trauma. Imagine inhaling a healing white light to the specific area that is experiencing pain or illness. On the exhale, imagine breathing out the pain, illness, or trauma. Inhale more healing- see this light carried within your breath, soothing this part of your body. If you have a tumor or inflammation, see this light shrinking the inflamed energy. Exhale out the disease, discomfort, or blocked energy. Continue this daily along with your medical treatment. If you are on medication, you can ask that your medication is blessed and that it be aligned with a full recovery. Instead of thinking of it as killing a disease, think of it as bringing your body into recovery and remission. Less fighting, more healing.

♦ Crystals for Health and Healing: Augelite, Turquoise, Smokey Quartz for clearing old energy, Clear Quartz, Citrine.

Chapter 11

Addiction and Mental Health

What I've found over the years is that most people experience addiction in some way, shape, or form. I personally have been in recovery for five and a half years at the time of writing this, and I am a big believer in twelve-step programs. Whether you feel called to a treatment program, or if you just want something to help you with your candy bar addiction or Netflix binging addiction, these prayers and mantras can help support you. One of the biggest tools I've seen help healing from addiction is being willing to look at how your addictive behavior is serving you. Most people focus solely on judging their behavior, which creates shame and guilt and ultimately perpetuates the cycle. When you can look at what your addictions are doing for you, you can start to see where the healing is needed. For example, many people use sugar as a way of grounding, soothing, or rewarding themselves for dealing with stressful circumstances. Knowing this gives you the power to say,

maybe I need a healthier stress management plan, maybe I need to get support, maybe I need a healthier reward system. Most addictions are a way of escaping, so looking at what you're escaping can be a powerful tool. Am I trying to escape myself? Am I trying to escape an uncomfortable situation? Am I trying to escape a relationship that I don't want to admit I'm unhappy in? A job? What are you running from? Sometimes it's an issue that you can face on your own with the support of Spirit, and sometimes it may be so many things that you'd benefit from the help of a counselor or support group. Regardless, being willing to look at the underlying issues can help give you clarity on the level of support you're needing. When I'm doing readings and see addiction or mental illness, my symbol is a bubble around the person's head. It means stuck in their own illness, not being able to see the bigger picture or other people's perspectives. A big tool in healing from addiction or mental illness is getting help with being able to see the bigger picture. Meditation is a great daily tool that helps bring you into more of a witness perspective and gives you a way to connect with Source energy to help you not feel so overwhelmed by life. Addiction, anxiety, depression, another mental illnesses usually include an element of wanting to control everything. This usually stems from a fear of feeling unsafe and needing to control everything and everyone which can cause massive anxiety and a lot of pressure. This can create overwhelm, and then we start to look for ways to disconnect or escape. These prayers and

mantras are designed to bring in Spiritual support to help with that overwhelm, bring a reminder that you are safe, release addictive patterns, and to release control over to your Higher Power. Mental illness and addiction, no matter how major or minor, creates a disconnection. Proper treatment needs to include a way of experiencing a connection with your Higher Power, your true self, and with others.

* Prayers, Affirmations, Mantras, and Visualizations *

God, please guide me towards the best treatment options. Please give me a sign that help is possible, and help me know who to reach out to. Amen.

Angels, please cut any and all cords connected to my past addictions. Please clear me of these behaviors and help me find healthy ways to manage my mind. Thank you! Amen.

God, I now surrender my entire life over to You. I see that in my controlling and managing, I have gotten off track, and I know that I can trust You to guide me back. Please take over and show me the way. I give up. Thank you.

God, please take this part of me that doesn't want to live anymore, this part of me that hurts so bad I can't put it into words, and please heal me. I am so sorry for turning away, please help me find my way back to myself, and to You. Help me remember who I really am and why I came here. Please clear me of all addictive behavior and show me what steps I need to take next. I trust You.

Spirit Team- I release to you my need to control everything around me. Please take over. Please help me see that everything is working out as it needs to. Please help me see that everyone is doing their best and help me focus on showing up as my best self. Thank you!

God, show me who You built me to be. Show me how You want me to deal with this situation.

God, help cleanse me of all anxiety, depression, obsession, worry, and fear. Please take these heavy loads off of my heart and soul and help me see the truth. Please help me to feel your love and safety. Thank you. Amen.

Angels, please take over this situation for me. Please help it all turn out in a way that's in everyone's highest and greatest good. Thank you. Amen.

I now choose to set myself free from this internal prison. I now seek the support and the help that I need to recover. I release all shame and guilt and give myself permission to heal fully. I know that I am safe and that God is supporting me.

I release my need to control others. I release my need to know all the details. I release my obsessions and worries. I trust that God is handling it and everything is working out. It's all okay. Everyone is doing the best that they know how to do, and it is not my job to fix them. I release them to the Universe and send them love and compassion.

I give myself permission to let go. I now surrender the struggle, the pain, and the fear. I surrender everything to the divine will. I trust in the bigger plan.

Visualizations:

Imagine a large white basket, the size of a hot air balloon basket, in front of you. Now imagine placing into this basket any people, situations, addictive substances or behaviors, fears, anything that you've been obsessing about. Place it all in the basket and then imagine sending the basket up to the Angels for them to sort out. Imagine the Angels standing all around you. As they surround you, they place their hands around you and create a cocoon of healing light. While in this light you know you are being protected. This is a safe place to come to anytime you feel overwhelmed, attacked, or afraid.

♦ Crystals for Recovery and Mental Health: Amethyst, Selenite, Blue Kyanite, Lithium Quartz, Lepidolite, Celestite

Chapter 12

Clarity: Making Clear, Confident Decisions

A lot of people struggle with feeling clear and confident in their decision making. I find that people will start to actually give their power of decision making over just to avoid self-doubt and the mental exhaustion that comes with trying to make the "best decision." People are influenced by external opinions and pressure, and try to either rationalize following their heart or fighting to convince their heart to get on board with their mind. It becomes this internal battle that causes a lot of people to freeze and not make any decision at all. The first step in clear decision making is to clear away all energy that's not yours. We've gone over several clearing techniques so any of those will work, or a simple "Please send all energy that's not mine back to where it came from with love and compassion. Thank you. "Next, getting quiet, connecting spiritually, and also grounding are all vital especially when it's a major decision. When I was deciding to leave my day job and do this work full time, I spent many

hours in prayer and meditation in one of my favorite sacred areas. I only made that choice when I felt calm and clear about it. When you're feeling connected and grounded, you can ask for guidance from your Spirit Team, and also check in and ask yourself what is truly in your best good. When you ask yourself questions in this calm, centered place, you can get clear answers. It's like you're able to drop into your heart or access your Soul because the mind is finally resting. This is the state you can enter to get your own intuitive guidance on situations. Of course, circumstances may still arise where you seek counsel with a spiritual advisor, mentor, or counselor, but for checking in and making decisions regularly this will help a lot!

* Prayers, Affirmations, Mantras, and Visualizations *

God, please help me make decisions in my highest and best good. Amen.

Angels, please help me make decisions from my higher self right now. Help me see the best action steps to take. Thank you! Spirit Team, help me feel what choice is in my best good here. Help me feel confident in my decision. Thank you!

I now make confident, clear decisions from a solid, centered place. I choose my next steps from my highest self. I trust that they are right for me.

I trust myself to choose powerfully. I know what to do and I give myself permission to act on it.

I am centered. I am calm. I now ask myself what decision to make and give myself permission to follow my heart.

I decide from a place of love, not fear.

Meditation:

Have a comfortable seat with your back straight. Your legs can be crossed or your feet can be flat on the ground, just make sure you are seated in a position that feels solid and you don't feel wobbly or uncomfortable. Take several moments breathing and aligning your body. Get yourself in a position that feels rooted, and then lengthen your spine and sit taller on every inhale. Ground and root into the ground on the exhale. Feel the support below you and feel your body lift and open up at the same time. Once you feel settled in, start to inhale light in through the crown of your head and exhale it out of your feet or pelvis. See this light filling you with divine clarity and support, and then rooting you into the earth below. Now, call upon your Angels and Guides or Spirit Team and ask that they join you in this meditation and help you see the best decisions possible. Imagine tuning into your heart. Bring your awareness to your heart, and see if you can access your higher self or your Soul-self from there. Your heart and your Soul-self will feel calm, connected, and light. When you have this peaceful feeling in your body, and feel this overall feeling of trust and like it's all okay, you've aligned with your

Soul self. From this state, ask yourself, what is in my best good here? What choice is in my highest good? Inquire about each possible decision and see what feels aligned and what feels heavy or off. Feel the energy of each decision in your body. The mind is quiet during this process, you're just feeling it. You can also grab a notebook and journal what comes to you during this time. When you feel confident in your next steps, thank your Spirit Team, thank yourself, thank God or the Universe, and take a few moments to integrate back into human form. You will most likely feel much more confident in your choices now!

◆ Crystals for making clear decisions: Any crystal that resonates with you most is good for this. Also, auralite, amethyst, red jasper. I like to combine a stone that helps me connect spiritually with a grounding stone. I'll hold one in each hand. For example, an amethyst with a citrine, or a Lemurian with a carnelian or Jasper. Bringing in both energies really helps you find that perfect balance.

Chapter 13

Raise Your Frequency

By now you've probably heard a lot of conversations and read a lot of books that talk about raising your vibration or tuning into a higher frequency. It's becoming a mainstream conversation, but a lot of people still don't fully understand what it means. I like the example of a radio station. If you think about an old-school radio where you'd have to turn the dial or on the newer radios if you hit scan and it goes from station to station. You are in charge of setting your "station" or tuning your "instrument" to the frequency/station/note you want it on. You can be programmed to complaining and victimhood, to prosperity and success, to love and gratitude, trust, etc. Whatever you want, but you are the one that decides where you want to operate from. The reason that these conversations are becoming so mainstream right now is because our whole planet is currently evolving and raising its frequency. A lot of people refer to this as the ascension process. Therefore, as the planet raises its frequency, people are either going into full-blown resistance and lowering their frequency causing a feeling of disconnection, or raising their

frequency along with it, causing them to feel more inflow and connected than ever before. Those people that are experiencing the flow are seeing numbers pop up that are special to them or that are master numbers. They are noticing that life is working in their favor, and things always work out. They are noticing synchronicities, a feeling of divine intervention and magic everywhere they go. The people experiencing disconnection are feeling left behind like life doesn't support them, like they just can't get ahead. Neither is wrong or bad nor is anything in between those extremes wrong or bad, it's simply a choice. That's all. If you want to experience the flow, peace, and connection, here are some prayers and mantras for raising your frequency, and some action steps you can take.

* Prayers, Affirmations, Mantras, and Visualizations *

God, please align me with Your divine light. Align me so that Your grace fills every area of my life and guides my every movement. Thank you! Amen.

Angels, please set me on a path that is in my highest and best good. Clear away all low vibration thoughts and attitudes, and help me feel grateful, positive, and joyful. Thank you!

Spirit Team, please set my energetic grid to one of love, abundance, success, and whatever else is in my highest and best good. Help lift my energy up to a frequency where I can feel you around me in all that I do. Awaken the holiness that flows through me. Thank you!

Universe, please lift me up to as high of a vibration as I can handle right now. Help me release all the old patterns and thoughts that do not align here, and replace them with higher frequency ways of being. Thank you!

I now function at a high frequency that is in alignment with my heart and soul. I adapt my mind and my thinking to this new frequency now. I release all resistance and fear. I trust that things are now working out in my favor.

I relax and allow life to flow through me. I trust that the Universe is always working for my best good. I am thankful. I am loving. I am generous.

I am at peace with the Universe. Everything is working out as it should.

Visualization:

Close your eyes and imagine yourself standing on a floor of brick or tiles. As you look out in front of you, to the sides of you, behind you, you see things that have happened in the past. You see yourself saying statements or thinking thoughts that aren't fully serving you or you see the reality that your past and current thoughts and beliefs have created. Notice how you feel here, in this reality. Try not to go into judgment or blame. Just have an awareness of what got you here, what's happened, what you're willing to leave behind. When you feel complete, like you've learned and you're ready for a new experience, say to

yourself: "I am now ready for a new life experience. I give my Angels and Spirit permission to raise my entire frequency mentally, spiritually, emotionally, and physically and guide me in creating a new life for myself. I am ready to be elevated. "As you give them permission, envision your Angels, or even just a bright light, lifting you up, off that floor, see that reality getting farther and farther away. See those thoughts and/or patterns sinking below you. Now, see yourself being brought up to a new floor. Maybe the flooring is bright white and radiant, maybe there's some grass or water. Regardless of what it looks like, it feels peaceful. Almost heavenly. Feel this divine light around you, supporting you and tuning you to this frequency. Tune into the peace, the trust, the safety, support, and love that's here. As you look around, see all experiences working out in your favor. See relationships being loving and healthy. See your physical health being at its best. See success and/or money coming your way. See opportunities being put in front of you as if you're the luckiest person alive. See yourself fully protected as though everyone and everything is going around you working to create all experiences to be in your best good. Working to help you. Say to yourself, "I now embrace this as my new reality. I am filled with love and gratitude. I see miracles and magic everywhere I go. The Universe is supporting my happiness. I receive blessings on a daily basis and I welcome happy experiences in my life.

Thank you." As you come back to your physical reality, imagine bringing this world you've created with you, and installing it into your energy field, seeing it radiate through your entire life like a shooting star going ahead of you, sprinkling stardust on all your experiences.

Rituals for Raising Your Frequency-

- Writing out a daily gratitude list.
- Daily meditation time.
- Listening to classical music, mantras, or music tuned to the frequency of 432 HZ or 528 HZ.
- Bathing or swimming in salt water.
- Adorning yourself in sacred oils and crystals.
- Eating clean, pure foods.
- Massaging yourself with oils and/or lotions, imagining sending love and light into your body as you do so. You can use essential oils mixed with jojoba, coconut oil, etc.
- Get your energy moving. Tapping, jumping up and down, dancing around. Something to get your energy moving will also raise your frequency instantly.
- Crystals for raising your frequency: Blue Kyanite paired with Citrine or Rose Quartz, Lemurian Quartz, Flourite, Celestite, Herkimer Diamond

♦ ♦ ♦

Chapter 14

Supportive Morning and Evening Rituals

How we begin our day and end our day is so important. In the morning we have an opportunity to set the tone for our entire day, to send out our intentions, to prepare our own energy and self for our day. In the evening, we have an opportunity to close our day on a good note, whether it was a good day or not. Evenings are great for reflecting, letting go, making note of anywhere we need to make shifts, and being grateful. When you take the time to start and end your day consciously you take your power back. It also helps to set aside the time to consciously call in your Spirit Team for support and guidance on a daily basis. Looking at morning and evening rituals can be intimidating. If you haven't been implementing a conscious routine, it can appear you don't have the time. Spirit would like to invite you to think about it from the perspective that you actually already have morning and evening rituals/routines. Maybe you just didn't consciously create them. If you bring your awareness into

these moments, you will probably find that you have more of a routine than you realize. Knowing this, ask yourself: Is this current routine setting me up for success in my life or not? If not, maybe try just implementing one specific thing from these lists. Don't overwhelm yourself by trying to do all of them, just try one at a time. See what works. Give it a week or two to see if you feel different or notice a shift. Changing doesn't have to be hard. Make it work for you. Below I am including small rituals and practices, one list is for the morning, one is for the evening. Feel free to modify these things to fit your life and beliefs.

Morning Rituals

*Happy Alarm Clock: Pick a song or tone that immediately puts you in a good mood. Alarm tones that sound like emergencies immediately send your nervous system into fight or flight as they jolt you awake. Try waking up in a supportive way.

*Visualizations: The morning is a great time to take 5-10 minutes visualizing either your specific goals coming in, a visualization from previous chapters, or even just visualizing how you want your day to go. Imagine sending out good vibes to everyone you're going to meet, the places you'll be, good vibes just paving the way for you.

*Affirmations and Mantras: Saying affirmations and mantras in the morning is a powerful way to consciously set your mind and thoughts to the frequency you want to be on

all day. I keep mine on sticky notes on my bathroom mirror and read them as I get ready.

*Prayer and Meditation: Taking time to pray and meditate will shift your life no matter what time of day you practice.

*Listen to happy music and wake your body up with some movement. Whether it's tapping, dancing around the house, or stretching, by listening to something upbeat and positive and moving, you're getting the energy in your body moving at the pace you choose for the day.

*Inviting your Spirit Team in: Invite them to accompany you and help you throughout your day. Talk to them about your desires, release any fears or worries, give them permission to help you.

*Bless your water, coffee, tea, or whatever else you consume first thing. Fill what you're consuming with love, health, and vitality and see it nourishing your body as you drink or eat it. Starting your day with a large glass of water is a great and healthy practice to implement, and will help keep you hydrated and energized.

*Remember your Why: Get your motivation flowing by remembering your Why for the day. The morning is all about setting your energy for the day, so if you need to be on your A-game, this a great one.

Evening Rituals

*Gratitude List: Write out 10 things you're grateful for from your day.

*Reflection: Write out and reflect on what went well and felt aligned during your day, and what felt off. Look at the things that felt off and try to see them from an open mind, and a place of un- attachment. Remind yourself that everyone is doing the best they can do at the time. Note any conversations you need to have to clear things up, any shifts you need to make, and then note all the things that went well from your day. Give yourself a moment to celebrate those things and experiences. Release it all to God, the Universe, and your Angels to take off your shoulders.

*Clear your energy: There are many clearing mantras and practices in previous chapters. Implementing any of those, saging yourself, or even just saying "Please send all energy that's not mine back to its originator with love and compassion," will do the trick. You can also listen to a guided meditation for clearing your energy too. There are some available to purchase at www.sarahreneeinc.com on the Store page.

*Invite your Angels and Spirit Team to do healing on you while you sleep. This is a nice one, especially after a hard day. Before bed, say a prayer and ask God, the Universe and its light, your Spirit Team, Angels, to do healing work on you. You can ask them to heal you, bring you back into balance and alignment, reset your energy grid, and help

repair your energy field so that you wake up feeling restored and rested.

*Write a letter to your Spirit Team: I used to write a letter to God every night in my journal. It's really helpful actually. They can read what you write, plus it's a great way to get things off your chest. Just don't store any journals with negativity under your bed. Keep them in the closet or get rid of them when you're done.

*Disconnect from electronics an hour before sleep: You can play some classical music, light some candles, read, write. Take sometime to consciously wind down before bed, you'll sleep much better.

*Self Care: The evenings are great for taking baths, relaxing, being quiet. Anything that feels nurturing and restoring to your soul.

*Crystals: You can use crystals to help you sleep and set the energy of your bed. You can also use them in the morning by either wearing them or holding them for a few minutes. There are plenty of resources to find crystals that will benefit you either online or in stores that carry them. I will usually sleep with a few under my pillow and also keep one under each corner of my mattress to hold the energy. Ultimately, simply by being conscious throughout your day gives you the power to maximize your life and well being. There is no need to overcomplicate things or make your schedule rigid and constrictive. Look at these tools as a way to support yourself at the start and end of your day.

A letter from Spirit and myself to You:

What spirit most wants you to know right now is that every single person has a magic inside of them. Your words, your thoughts, and your actions are how that magic is expressed. Rituals don't have to be connected to a religion or the occult. Routines don't have to be rigid and challenging. Faith doesn't have to be followed or found outside of yourself. You are the church. You are the temple, the messenger, the practitioner, the sacred, holy being. When I bring through people from the afterlife, a lot of them bring up that too many people spend time arguing about faith, spirituality, and religion, and not enough time living it. They say that all the religions were really created as a guide to put people in touch with God, Source, and the Universe. These prayers and mantras were written to be inclusive of all belief systems, and you are free to adjust any wording to make it aligned with your specific beliefs. The most important thing is that you know that you were created on purpose, that you have an energy that is greater than you watching over you, guiding you, and wanting to support you, and that you are loved beyond your wildest imagination. They watch over you and just glow with joy seeing you learn your lessons, bounce back after falls, helping others, being happy and thankful. Spirit wants you to enjoy your life, and to know that you are never alone. This book is meant to help support that.

To help support you in finding your inner connection with Spirit and nurturing that connection daily. It is meant to help you bring this connection, this divinity, into all areas of your life. It is meant to put you in touch with your inner magic and holiness. You are extraordinary. I love you. Thank you so much for being here.

Author Bio

Sarah Renee is an international psychic medium, which means she has been given the gift from God to connect with the other side. Sarah brings through messages from people who have died, as well as from the Angels, and a higher consciousness that she refers to as the Guides. Sarah has helped thousands of people find closure, clarity, peace of mind, and their purpose. Sarah is also a Spiritual Transformation Coach, Teacher, Minister, and Best Selling Author. She has served a diverse range of people, from

powerful CEO's, entrepreneurs, and celebrities, to fire fighters, law enforcement, stay at home moms, troubled teens, young kids who have lost siblings or parents, ex-cons who are trying to get back on their feet, and everyone in between. She is currently based out of sunny San Diego- but sees clients from all over the world through virtual or phone sessions. She specializes in two types of readings. One is when she connects with your deceased loved ones. Sarah brings through messages from loved ones on the other side in order to validate that it is in fact them, and to bring much needed closure and peace of mind. She also specializes in more of a spiritual coaching format, where she brings through messages from the Guides and Angels in order to help provide people clarity, find happiness, and live their best life possible. She has single session rates, group rates, one on one coaching programs, and online group classes.

You can learn more and schedule your session with her at www.sarahreneeinc.com or email directly at sarahrenee444@gmail.com.